I0815087

CHEERLEADING

CHEER SKILLS AND DRILLS

By India James

SportsZone
An Imprint of Abdo Publishing
abdobooks.com

abdobooks.com

Printed in China
052024
092024

Cover Photo: John Korduner/Icon Sportswire/AP Images
Interior Photos: Shutterstock Images, 4–5; Lynnette Peizer/Alamy, 6; Andy Mead/YCJ/Icon Sportswire/AP Images, 8–9; Seth Goldfarb/Stone/Getty Images, 11; Image Source/Getty Images, 12; Alex Potemkin/E+/Getty Images, 14–15; Jerome Davis/Icon Sportswire/AP Images, 17; Corey Perrine/Naples Daily News/AP Images, 19; Zia Soleil/Stone/Getty Images, 20–21; iStockphoto, 22, 26; Simonkr/E+/Getty Images, 24–25; Tony Anderson/Stone/Getty Images, 29

Editor: Christa Kelly
Series Designer: Kate Liestman

Library of Congress Control Number: 2023949288

Library of Congress Cataloging-in-Publication Data

Names: James, India, author.
Title: Cheer skills and drills / by India James
Description: Minneapolis, Minnesota: Abdo Publishing, 2025 | Series: Cheerleading | Includes online resources and index.
Identifiers: ISBN 9781098293499 (lib. bdg.) | ISBN 9798384912767 (ebook)
Subjects: LCSH: Cheerleading--Juvenile literature. | Skills training--Juvenile literature. | Sports--Juvenile literature.
Classification: DDC 791.6--dc23

TABLE OF CONTENTS

CHAPTER 1

CHEERLEADING

Cheerleading is a fun and energetic activity. It is an amazing display of dance, gymnastics, and stunts. There are many different types of cheerleaders. Some are part of school teams. These cheerleaders perform on the sidelines of school games. Other cheerleaders belong to All Star teams. These organizations often compete against other cheerleading squads. Still others are professional cheerleaders.

Cheerleading is a great way to stay active.

These cheerleaders entertain crowds during big sports games.

No matter who they perform with, cheerleaders awe crowds with their incredible routines. Routines are choreographed performances created by

Cheerleaders typically train multiple times each week.

coaches, choreographers, or cheerleaders. They're made up of individual skills and often paired with music.

It takes a lot of hard work and dedication to perform cheerleading routines. Cheerleaders have to be strong, flexible, and energetic. They must also know the many jumps, tumbling skills, and stunts that their team performs. Learning the moves that make up routines is one of the first steps toward becoming a cheerleader.

CHEERLEADING IN THE UNITED STATES

Cheerleading is one of the most popular activities in the United States. There are about 3 million cheerleaders in the country. Most are girls, but cheerleaders can be any gender.

CHAPTER 2

STUNTS

Stunts are among the most popular cheerleading moves. A stunt is a skill in which a cheerleader is supported above the ground by one or more of their teammates. High above the ground, a cheerleader can hold a pose or be launched into the air to perform tricks.

Stunts can be dangerous. However, when performed correctly, they show off a cheerleader's strength and skill. They can also captivate any audience.

When performing stunts, safety should be a cheerleader's top priority.

STUNT POSITIONS

Stunts involve at least two people. Each person has a role and a title. The person supported above the ground is called the flyer. The person supporting the flyer is called the base. The base holds on to the flyer's feet to keep the stunt stable.

Most stunts include a back spot. This person is responsible for making sure the flyer's head and shoulders stay safe. They're charged with catching and protecting the flyer's neck and head when the stunt comes down. The back spot also helps launch the flyer into the air and supports the stunt by holding the flyer's ankles.

There are two different types of stunts. One is called a single. This is when the flyer has people supporting only one leg. A double is when the flyer has people supporting both legs.

PERFORMING STUNTS

To start a stunt, the flyer jumps. The bases then lift the flyer into the air. Bases should start with their feet shoulder-width apart. Their hands should be on the flyer's hips or legs. The bases should begin lifting with their legs, followed by their shoulders.

Flyers should always look out at the audience, not down at the ground.

They should hold the flyer's feet at the shoulder height or above their heads. Once the flyer is in position, the bases lock their arms.

In a double stunt, each base holds one of the flyer's feet. The flyer must keep their ankles, hips, and shoulders aligned. Keeping these joints straight

It's important for flyers to learn how to fall safely.

and tight will keep the flyer's weight divided equally between each base. This helps keep the stunt balanced and safe.

Once the stunt is in position, the flyer either holds a pose or performs tricks in the air. To start a flying trick, the flyer is tossed into the air by the bases. Then the flyer performs a tumbling skill or a jump before being caught by the bases.

At the end of each stunt, the flyer must come down. This is called a dismount. Flyers often dismount through what is called a cradle. This is a move in which the bases catch the flyer's legs and back. Flips, tricks, and turns while a flyer is falling into the cradle make the dismount one of the most thrilling parts of a performance. It's important for the flyer to end the dismount with their legs straight, hips slightly bent, and body facing up. This position makes it easier for the bases and the back spot to catch the flyer. Once the flyer has landed in the cradle, they can stand up.

PYRAMIDS

Pyramids are popular in cheerleading. A pyramid is a skill in which several stunts combine to make one big stunt. Flyers can hold hands to connect the stunts. Sometimes an additional flyer is launched into the pyramid to act as a bridge between the cheerleaders.

CHAPTER 3

TUMBLING

Tumbling helps make cheerleading exciting. Tumbling skills are gymnastics moves performed without any extra equipment. These moves include rolls, cartwheels, and roundoffs. They also include advanced skills such as handsprings.

Tumbling requires strength, practice, and courage. Whether performed on the ground or in the air as part of a stunt, tumbling is a major part of cheerleading.

Tumbling requires cheerleaders to be fast, strong, and flexible.

BASIC TUMBLING MOVES

One of the simplest tumbling skills is the roll. Rolls can be forward or backward. Cheerleaders perform these moves by tucking their chins to their chests and rolling. The cartwheel is another basic tumbling skill. Roundoffs are similar to cartwheels, but the cheerleaders land with their feet together.

Rolls, cartwheels, and roundoffs are some of the most basic tumbling moves in cheerleading, but they can combine with other skills to make an exciting routine. Tumbling elements are often done

TUMBLE TRACKS

Some coaches have cheerleaders practice new moves on a tumble track. A tumble track is a long trampoline with cushioned sides. This gives the cheerleaders enough room to try a series of skills.

Learning complex tumbling skills takes patience.

in series or done by a group in unison. Synchronized tumbling makes routines look clean and practiced.

LEARNING TUMBLING

Tumbling can be dangerous. It's important to learn these skills in a safe environment. Having proper equipment and experienced teachers will help a cheerleader learn more advanced moves. It's always a good idea to learn tumbling skills in a class.

A tumbling instructor may have cheerleaders try out new skills on a trampoline. Trampolines help cheerleaders gain confidence on a safe, springy floor before moving to a harder surface. It's important for cheerleaders to move to a performance surface only when an instructor agrees they are ready. Performing skills on a hard surface such as grass or a carpet will require more strength and faster movements than doing the same skills on a trampoline.

STRETCHING AND EXERCISING FOR TUMBLING

Stretching is an important part of keeping muscles and joints healthy. It helps muscles stay flexible. Cheerleaders need to regularly stretch their shoulders, arms, backs, legs, and hips.

Stretching before and after practicing or performing can help prevent injuries.

Exercising is another way cheerleaders keep their bodies strong and healthy. Cheerleaders exercise to strengthen the muscles they use while performing. Tumbling requires a lot of core strength. To strengthen their cores, cheerleaders can do exercises that build back and stomach muscles.

Stretching after workouts helps muscles recover.

CHAPTER 4

JUMPS

Cheerleaders perform many jumps during their routines. One popular jump is the toe touch. During a toe touch, cheerleaders jump and spread their legs in a V shape while reaching their hands toward their heels. Reaching for the heels rather than the toes makes the stretch look deeper.

The pike is another popular jump. To do a pike, cheerleaders jump with both

It takes strength and flexibility to perform jumps with proper form.

Chiefs

legs extended straight out in front of their chests while reaching their hands toward their heels.

LEARNING TO JUMP

Form is one of the most important parts of any jump. Cheerleaders should have their chests raised, toes pointed, and heads up. During competitions, judges will be looking for cheerleaders to have good form. Maintaining proper form earns teams

Jumps performed one after another are called combination jumps.

more points. It also helps a team's routine look clean and synchronized.

Some jumps, such as pikes and toe touches, can be practiced while sitting. Cheerleaders can sit on the ground and practice holding the right pose. This can help cheerleaders perfect their moves during jumps.

When cheerleaders are finishing jumps, they should always land with their feet together and knees bent. This prevents injuries caused by landing with too much weight on one foot. They should also always land in one motion, without taking any extra steps after hitting the ground.

PREPARING FOR JUMPS

Cheerleaders need to stay fit to be able to do complex jumps. Jumps take a lot of energy. It's important for cheerleaders to build endurance. Jogging and biking are ways to build stamina.

Jumps also take leg strength. Cheerleaders build strength by doing exercises. Burpees are an exercise that builds leg strength. A burpee is a push-up followed by a jump. Exercises such as burpees help cheerleaders build the endurance and strength they need to perform successful jumps.

CHAPTER 5

DANCE

Many common dance moves can be found in cheerleading routines. Dance moves help bring a routine together. They add style and help connect stunts, tumbling skills, and jumps.

HANDS

Hands play an important role in cheerleading dance moves. Sometimes the athletes hold props while they dance. Props include megaphones, pom-poms,

Cheerleaders have to learn dozens of dance moves.

Cheerleaders often use pom-poms while they dance to accentuate their movements.

and flags. Cheerleaders hold props to add style and excitement to their routines.

When cheerleaders aren't holding props, they keep their hands in two main positions. The first is the blade position. In the blade position, a cheerleader's fingers are extended and pressed tightly against each other. Fists are the other most common hand position. Cheerleaders also clap and clasp their hands during routines. In both positions, the cheerleaders' arms should be against their bodies.

ARMS

Arm motions are another important part of any routine. A high V is one of the first moves a cheerleader learns. During a high V, both arms are raised and positioned slightly away from the cheerleader's body. The move looks like the cheerleader is making a V with their arms. A low V is similar to a high V. In this move, the cheerleader's arms extend down and slightly away from their body.

There are several other positions named after the letter they resemble. In the T position, the cheerleader's arms are extended straight out from their body. In the K position, one of the cheerleader's arms crosses their body and is angled down. The other arm moves diagonally up and away from their body.

Punches are another common cheerleading move. During a punch, one arm is raised directly over the cheerleader's shoulder. The other arm is bent with the hand on the cheerleader's hip. A touchdown is almost the same but with both arms extended.

Once cheerleaders have the basic motions memorized, it's important that they get comfortable performing the moves. Cheerleaders can do this by practicing in front of a mirror. Cheerleaders should also practice with their teams. Teams need to practice performing in unison.

Cheerleading is a fun and athletic activity. It combines stunts, tumbling skills, jumps, and dance moves to create routines that can make a crowd go wild. With enough practice and dedication, a cheerleader can learn to perform even the most complicated routines.

Dance moves such as high Vs can be combined with stunts.

GLOSSARY

choreographed
Something that has been planned, often referring to a routine.

choreographer
Someone who creates routines for dancers or cheerleaders.

core
The middle section of the body, including the chest and back.

endurance
A person's ability to keep doing something.

form
The way movements and skills are performed.

megaphone
A cone-shaped prop used to make someone's voice louder.

pom-pom
A ball-shaped prop usually made of shiny pieces of plastic or foil.

prop
An object such as a pom-pom, flag, or megaphone that is used to enhance a cheerleader's routine.

routine
A performance made up of individual stunts, tumbling moves, jumps, and dance moves.

series
Moves performed one after another.

stamina
The ability to perform physical exercise for an extended time.

synchronized
Performed at the same time as another person.

unison
Performed by a group at the same time.

MORE INFORMATION

BOOKS

Banks, Anita. *Cheer Tryouts and Training*. Abdo, 2025.

Letkeman, Candice. *Cheerleading Basics*. AV2 by Weigl, 2020.

Moffatt, Ali, and Alana Potter. *The Cheerleading Book: The Young Athlete's Guide*. Firefly, 2020.

ONLINE RESOURCES

To learn more about cheer skills and drills, please visit abdobooklinks.com or scan this QR code. These links are routinely monitored and updated to provide the most current information available.

INDEX

ABOUT THE AUTHOR

India James writes nonfiction for young readers. She loves learning and writing about new things. James lives in Ohio with her family.